A LITTLE REES SPECHT CULTIVATES KINDNESS

Story by RICHARD E. SPECHT, JR.

Illustrations by ADAM D. SMITH

CREDITS

Written by Richard E. Specht, Jr. | Illustration and Design by Adam D. Smith | Assistant Art Direction by Sarah Durinick
Text Copyright © 2014 by Richard E. Specht, Jr. | Illustrations Copyright © 2014 by Adam D. Smith

Editor: Beth Williams | Proof Reader: Lauren Dwyer Lowther

ISBN: 978-0-692-25523-0

FOR MY LITTLE REES:

"Kindness is like a seed that can only grow and spread if it is cultivated through a respect for life... "

-Richard E. Specht Jr.

One day, while out riding his favorite tractor, Trakta, Little Rees Specht stopped in his field to see how his crops were growing.

He looked around at his field
full of fruits and vegetables, amazed that
only a few months earlier they were
nothing more than tiny seeds.

Little Rees Specht smiled. He recalled the constant
care and watering of his seeds that turned a dirty field
of mud and stones into a thriving garden.
The beautiful and delicious fruits and vegetables
were now ready for harvesting.

On harvest day, Little Rees Specht and all of his friends carefully gathered the fruits and vegetables and placed them in baskets to be taken to the market to sell.

With all of the fruits and vegetables packed, Little Rees Specht thanked his friends for their help as he and Trakta made their way to the market.

On the way to the market,
Little Rees Specht spotted a girl
named Kaylee. Kaylee was on the
side of the road next to her broken
bike, and she was crying.

Little Rees Specht stopped Trakta and picked up Kaylee.
"Why are you crying?" he asked.

"My bike hit a rock and my handlebars
came off! It's too far to walk to town
and I need to be at Abby's Bakery
to deliver my cookies," she said.

"Don't worry, Kaylee, I can fix your handlebars," said Little Rees Specht. He grabbed his toolbox from Trakta and carefully chose the tools he needed to fix the bike.

After a few minutes, Little Rees Specht tightened the last bolt and checked to make sure the handlebars were tight.

#AJO

"Here, you go Kaylee, good as new,"
Little Rees Specht proclaimed.
"Now you can make it to the bake shop!"

Kaylee thanked him and went on her way to the bakery.
Little Rees Specht smiled and waved goodbye, not knowing
that his kind deed had just planted a different kind of seed...

...the seed of kindness.

As Kaylee rode her bike to the bake shop she noticed a little boy named Gavin crying in his front yard. Gavin was upset because try as he might, he could not capture the rainbow in the sky to give to his brother, Brian.

Kaylee knew that she could help Gavin, just as Little Rees Specht had helped her. She handed him two of her rainbow cookies. "Take one rainbow cookie for yourself, and share one with your brother, Brian," she said.

...and the seed grew.

Gavin could not believe his eyes! The very nice girl,
Kaylee, had given him the rainbow he was chasing.
Because of Kaylee's generosity he had a
rainbow to give to his brother!

Gavin was so excited to tell Brian all about Kaylee and give him one of the rainbow cookies. As he walked over to Brian, he thought about how Kaylee's kindness had helped him catch his rainbow.

He wanted Brian to feel as happy as he did, so instead of one cookie, he gave Brian both cookies!

...and the seed grew more.

Later that day, Brian was out shopping with his mommy when he met Kieran who was sad that he didn't have enough money saved for the action figure he wanted.

Remembering how good it felt to get the cookies from his brother, Brian gave Kieran the money he had in his pocket so he could buy the toy.

...and the seed grew more.

Kieran was thrilled
with his new toy!
He played with his
super action man the
whole day and took it
everywhere he went.

As he and his mommy drove
home, Kieran spotted a
toy drive at the local firehouse,
and it gave him an idea:

*Maybe I can make someone
else as happy as that nice little
boy Brian made me,* he thought.

Kieran asked his mommy to stop at the firehouse. He donated his stuffed teddy to the drive, smiling, as he knew some little boy or girl would be as happy as he was to have a teddy to love.

...and the seed grew more.

A young girl named Jessie stopped by the toy drive with her daddy. Jessie could not believe her luck! She saw a teddy bear that was just like her lost teddy, Bearsie. As Jessie and her daddy made their way to the harvest festival she hugged and squeezed her new teddy, promising never to lose him again.

"I never thought I would see Bearsie ever again, Daddy," said Jessie smiling.

"I told you if you never, ever, give up, anything is possible," replied her daddy.

Thanks to Kieran's donation, Jessie was very happy. She decided to make someone else just as happy and volunteered to help unpack fruits and vegetables at the harvest fair.

...and the seed became a beautiful flower that could now make seeds of its own.

Miss Lorilei, the owner of the market that ran the harvest fair, could not hold back her smile. Never before had she witnessed such kindness! It seemed like everyone from town was lending a helping hand, even little Jessie who couldn't hold more than a few fruits and vegetables at a time! Miss Lorilei thought and thought about how she could repay everyone for their kindness. An idea began to sprout in her head...

What better way to repay everyone's hard work than to supply the seeds for next year's harvest, thought Miss Lorilei. With that, she donated bags of seeds to all the Farmers who brought their fruits and vegetables to the market, including Little Rees Specht.

...and a new seed was sown, created from the harvest of kindness that Little Rees Specht cultivated.

Little Rees Specht jumped for joy! Because of Miss Lorilei's kindness, he would be able to plant even more seeds for next year's harvest!

Grinning widely, Little Rees Specht hopped back on Trakta and began to make his way home. On the way, he witnessed something he did not expect:

He saw Jessie, smiling, cuddling a bear and thanking Kieran.
He saw Kieran flying his super action man with one hand and waving thanks
to Brian with the other.

He saw Brian hugging his brother Gavin, and he saw Gavin grinning and
thanking Kaylee for the rainbow cookies.

Suddenly, Little Rees Specht realized that everything that had happened that day had started with his original act of kindness...

...and just like every other seed he had ever planted, that kindness only needed a Little Rees Specht to help it grow and spread!

THE END... The Beginning

YOU have been **given** a **seed** of kindness...

...with the **help** of a little **Rees Specht.**

YOU have been **given** a **seed** of kindness...

...with the **help** of a little **Rees Specht.**

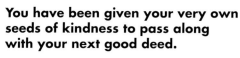

You have been given your very own seeds of kindness to pass along with your next good deed.

Carefully cut them out with an adult and f Like facebook.com/ReesSpechtLife

WATCH, SHARE and SEE the many ways these seeds can grow!

YOU have been **given** a **seed** of kindness...

...with the **help** of a little **Rees Specht.**

YOU have been **given** a **seed** of kindness...

...with the **help** of a little **Rees Specht.**

YOU have been **given** a **seed** of kindness...

...with the **help** of a little **Rees Specht.**

YOU have been **given** a **seed** of kindness...

...with the **help** of a little **Rees Specht.**

YOU have been **given** a **seed** of kindness...

...with the **help** of a little **Rees Specht.**

YOU have been **given** a **seed** of kindness...

...with the **help** of a little **Rees Specht.**

YOU have been **given** a **seed** of kindness...

...with the **help** of a little **Rees Specht.**

YOU have been **given** a **seed** of kindness...

...with the **help** of a little **Rees Specht.**

YOU have been **given** a **seed** of kindness...

...with the **help** of a little **Rees Specht.**

cultivate kindness

Your kindness is needed to help this seed sprout. Pass this card along with your next kind act and watch the seed grow. Every little seed you plant has the potential to make this a kinder world, one Rees' piece at a time.

cultivate kindness

Your kindness is needed to help this seed sprout. Pass this card along with your next kind act and watch the seed grow. Every little seed you plant has the potential to make this a kinder world, one Rees' piece at a time.

cultivate kindness

Your kindness is needed to help this seed sprout. Pass this card along with your next kind act and watch the seed grow. Every little seed you plant has the potential to make this a kinder world, one Rees' piece at a time.

cultivate kindness

Your kindness is needed to help this seed sprout. Pass this card along with your next kind act and watch the seed grow. Every little seed you plant has the potential to make this a kinder world, one Rees' piece at a time.

cultivate kindness

Your kindness is needed to help this seed sprout. Pass this card along with your next kind act and watch the seed grow. Every little seed you plant has the potential to make this a kinder world, one Rees' piece at a time.

cultivate kindness

Your kindness is needed to help this seed sprout. Pass this card along with your next kind act and watch the seed grow. Every little seed you plant has the potential to make this a kinder world, one Rees' piece at a time.

cultivate kindness

Your kindness is needed to help this seed sprout. Pass this card along with your next kind act and watch the seed grow. Every little seed you plant has the potential to make this a kinder world, one Rees' piece at a time.

cultivate kindness

Your kindness is needed to help this seed sprout. Pass this card along with your next kind act and watch the seed grow. Every little seed you plant has the potential to make this a kinder world, one Rees' piece at a time.

cultivate kindness

Your kindness is needed to help this seed sprout. Pass this card along with your next kind act and watch the seed grow. Every little seed you plant has the potential to make this a kinder world, one Rees' piece at a time.

cultivate kindness

Your kindness is needed to help this seed sprout. Pass this card along with your next kind act and watch the seed grow. Every little seed you plant has the potential to make this a kinder world, one Rees' piece at a time.

cultivate kindness

Your kindness is needed to help this seed sprout. Pass this card along with your next kind act and watch the seed grow. Every little seed you plant has the potential to make this a kinder world, one Rees' piece at a time.

YOU have been **given** a **seed** of kindness...

...with the **help** of a little **Rees Specht.**

YOU have been **given** a **seed** of kindness...

...with the **help** of a little **Rees Specht.**

YOU have been **given** a **seed** of kindness...

...with the **help** of a little **Rees Specht.**

YOU have been **given** a **seed** of kindness...

...with the **help** of a little **Rees Specht.**

YOU have been **given** a **seed** of kindness...

...with the **help** of a little **Rees Specht.**

YOU have been **given** a **seed** of kindness...

...with the **help** of a little **Rees Specht.**

YOU have been **given** a **seed** of kindness...

...with the **help** of a little **Rees Specht.**

YOU have been **given** a **seed** of kindness...

...with the **help** of a little **Rees Specht.**

YOU have been **given** a **seed** of kindness...

...with the **help** of a little **Rees Specht.**

YOU have been **given** a **seed** of kindness...

...with the **help** of a little **Rees Specht.**

YOU have been **given** a **seed** of kindness...

...with the **help** of a little **Rees Specht.**

YOU have been **given** a **seed** of kindness...

...with the **help** of a little **Rees Specht.**

cultivate kindness

Your kindness is needed to help this seed sprout. Pass this card along with your next kind act and watch the seed grow. Every little seed you plant has the potential to make this a kinder world, one Rees' piece at a time.

facebook.com/ReesSpechtLife www.ReesSpechtLife.com

cultivate kindness

Your kindness is needed to help this seed sprout. Pass this card along with your next kind act and watch the seed grow. Every little seed you plant has the potential to make this a kinder world, one Rees' piece at a time.

facebook.com/ReesSpechtLife www.ReesSpechtLife.com

cultivate kindness

Your kindness is needed to help this seed sprout. Pass this card along with your next kind act and watch the seed grow. Every little seed you plant has the potential to make this a kinder world, one Rees' piece at a time.

facebook.com/ReesSpechtLife www.ReesSpechtLife.com

cultivate kindness

Your kindness is needed to help this seed sprout. Pass this card along with your next kind act and watch the seed grow. Every little seed you plant has the potential to make this a kinder world, one Rees' piece at a time.

facebook.com/ReesSpechtLife www.ReesSpechtLife.com

cultivate kindness

Your kindness is needed to help this seed sprout. Pass this card along with your next kind act and watch the seed grow. Every little seed you plant has the potential to make this a kinder world, one Rees' piece at a time.

facebook.com/ReesSpechtLife www.ReesSpechtLife.com

cultivate kindness

Your kindness is needed to help this seed sprout. Pass this card along with your next kind act and watch the seed grow. Every little seed you plant has the potential to make this a kinder world, one Rees' piece at a time.

facebook.com/ReesSpechtLife www.ReesSpechtLife.com

cultivate kindness

Your kindness is needed to help this seed sprout. Pass this card along with your next kind act and watch the seed grow. Every little seed you plant has the potential to make this a kinder world, one Rees' piece at a time.

facebook.com/ReesSpechtLife www.ReesSpechtLife.com

cultivate kindness

Your kindness is needed to help this seed sprout. Pass this card along with your next kind act and watch the seed grow. Every little seed you plant has the potential to make this a kinder world, one Rees' piece at a time.

facebook.com/ReesSpechtLife www.ReesSpechtLife.com

cultivate kindness

Your kindness is needed to help this seed sprout. Pass this card along with your next kind act and watch the seed grow. Every little seed you plant has the potential to make this a kinder world, one Rees' piece at a time.

facebook.com/ReesSpechtLife www.ReesSpechtLife.com

cultivate kindness

Your kindness is needed to help this seed sprout. Pass this card along with your next kind act and watch the seed grow. Every little seed you plant has the potential to make this a kinder world, one Rees' piece at a time.

cultivate kindness

Your kindness is needed to help this seed sprout. Pass this card along with your next kind act and watch the seed grow. Every little seed you plant has the potential to make this a kinder world, one Rees' piece at a time.

cultivate kindness

Your kindness is needed to help this seed sprout. Pass this card along with your next kind act and watch the seed grow. Every little seed you plant has the potential to make this a kinder world, one Rees' piece at a time.

facebook.com/ReesSpechtLife

Suggestions for planting your own seed of kindness and leaving your card:

1. Write letters of appreciation to groups that are taking the time to help others, such as **#AJO** www.ajoforever.com, to let them know you support them and appreciate what they do!

2. Bring in **your neighbor's** garbage pails/mail/newspapers.

3. **Start a meal plan** for a family that has suffered a tragedy.

4. **Volunteer** at a food pantry/homeless shelter

5. **Visit** a retirement home. Color a picture to give to someone there.

6. Help support foundations like **NEGU** (Never Ever Give Up: The Jessie Rees Foundation) and help children fighting cancer. www.NEGU.org

7. Do an **unexpected chore** that your parents did not ask you to do.

8. **Donate** unused toys to a local toy drive/children's charity

9. While waiting in line, **let someone go** ahead of you.

10. Put change in a vending machine, or tape an envelope with change to it, and **pay for the next person's** snack or drink.

11. **Send cookies or food** to a local firehouse/EMT group to say: **"Thank you for all you do!"**

12. **Buy a "Suspended Coffee"** for someone who does not have money to buy one for themselves! www.suspendedcoffees.com

13. **Start a "Kindness Jar"** to collect loose change and then donate the money once a year to a charity.

14. **Buy flowers** and take them to a local hospital and give them to someone who has not had a visitor.

15. **Offer a seat** you are sitting in to someone who could use it more than you.

16. **Leave a book** you have already read somewhere like a hospital or church for another person to enjoy.

17. **Volunteer** your time at a non-profit organization such as: **The Smithtown Children's Foundation.** www.smithtownchildrensfoundation.com

www.SmithtownChildrensFoundation.com

18. **Hold the door** for someone.

19. Write out a **"Thank you note"** to someone who helped you with anything.

20. **Say something nice** to someone for no other reason than to make them smile.

21. **Help start a fundraiser**/raise awareness for worthy cause such as: **The Long Island Drowning Prevention Task Force.** www.LIDPTF.org

A ReesSpechtful Thank You to our Partners in Spreading the Seeds of Kindnes_

Lessons For Life
"Where Children Learn to Love & Respect the Water"

1-866-SAFE-SWIM • www.saf-t-swim.com

Matthew's Giving Tree Foundation

The mission of Matthew's Giving Tree Foundation is simply to help families provide the best quality of life for their children who live with disabilities and challenges. www.matthewsgivingtree.com

— A Special Thank You to our Business Sponsors —

All Type Collision & Repairs, Inc.
218 48th Street
Brooklyn, NY 11220
(718) 492-8143
all-type-collision-and-repairs.com

J&C graphics

JC Graphics
230 Knickerbocker Ave
Bohemia, NY 11716
(631) 319-6919
www.jc-graphics.net

RAUL E NEW YORK
by Silvana Penavic
www.raulenewyork.com

USED PIANO GALLERY
A DIVISION OF STEINWAY & SONS

Steinway Used Piano Gallery of Long Island
505 Walt Whitman Road
Melville, NY 11747
(631) 424-0525
www.usedpianogallery.com

INTERSTATE
Home Loan Center, Inc.

Interstate Home Loan Center, Inc.
Alex J. Niven, President
(631) 393-6018
www.myequityloan.com

SENIOR Helpers
Care and comfort at a moment's notice.

Senior Helpers of Smithtown
Gayle Lindroth, President
308 West Main Street, Suite 202
Smithtown, NY 11787
(631) 979-5540
seniorhelpers.com/smithtown

COHEN'S Fashion Optical

Cohen's Fashion Optical
755 Old Country Road
Riverhead, NY 11901
(631) 727-3173
www.cohensfashionoptical.com/
store/755-old-country-rd-riverhead-ny

— Thank you to the following schools for helping us plant the seeds of kindness —

Tackan Elementary School – Nesconset, NY • Branch Brook Elementary School – Smithtown, NY • Sunrise Drive Elementary School – Sayville, NY

— Thank you to the following families for helping to cultivate kindness in Rees' name —

The O'Leary Family | Theresa and Christopher Beck and Family | Emma Marino and Family | Susan Hazen and Family
Dorothy Damiano and Family | Jill Smith and Family | The Damm Family: Monica, Kevin, Eric, and Jesse | The Lindroth Family
My Mother, Janet Specht. I love you Mom. Rees will always love his Oma.
My amazing wife, Samantha. You are my rock. My heart. My soul. I will always love you.